OFFICIAL GUIDE
TO SELLING
INSURANCE

For New Agents

DAVID DUFORD

Table of Contents

A Note On How I Write, And How This Book Is Designed

Let me lay some groundwork before proceeding.

First, I write like I talk. Don't expect an Ivy-League compendium. Just simple, easy-to-understand language on selling insurance for new agents.

Second, this book is NOT an academic study on selling insurance. You will find no graphs, charts, or references here.

My singular goal is to communicate my experiences as a personal producer and recruiter to over 1,000 agents as to how the insurance business works, what career landmines to avoid, and how to determine the best course of action in your insurance selling career.

Have questions, thoughts, or criticisms? I welcome them all. You can reach me directly at david@davidduford.com.

Introduction
About David Duford

Here's a little bit about myself.

I am the owner and operator of DavidDuford.com.

I specialize in recruiting agents and agencies to become top producers utilizing proven sales and marketing systems in either of the following insurance products/markets:

- Final Expense (Face-To-Face and Tele sales),
- Annuities,
- Mortgage Protection,
- Medicare Supplements.
- Medicare Advantage, and
- Indexed Universal Life (IULs)

Humble Beginnings In Selling Insurance

I started my insurance career in 2011, jumping into the final expense business as an act of desperation.

Why? Because my existing business in the personal training industry was going down the tubes financially due to the negative economic factors of the Great Recession.

I've had my ups and downs in the insurance business. Early on, I failed out and had to take a job elsewhere, largely due to my own shortcomings and immaturity in not following what the experts recommend as their preferred sales and marketing strategy. Luckily, I got my head back on straight, and went back full-time into final expense insurance 12 months after I originally left the business.

Fast-forward to present day, Things are rocking along!

I have recruited more than 1,000 agents, teaching them how to sell final expense, annuities, mortgage protection, and Medicare Supplements, Medicare Advantage, and IULs, following the same system of success I employed throughout my career as a personal producer.

Many of my agents have developed into six-income earners following this same model of success.

"Hardest Working Man In Insurance"

In addition to helping agents daily become successful personal producers in my agency, I also do the following:

Operate a highly-successful YouTube Channel with over 1,000 videos, netting over 50,000 views monthly and growing, and projected to hit 10,000 subscribers by November 2019. Make sure you subscribe for my daily videos, live stream podcasts, and top agent interviews.

I've written two best-selling insurance sales books – The Official Guide To Selling Final Expense, and Interviews With Top Producing Insurance Agents.

I write a TON of highly-read insurance sales training content on my blog found at davidduford.com.

I contribute written and video content to LinkedIn, the Insurance Selling Magazine, Reviews.com, and the Insurance Forum.

Publish a daily "No BS David Duford Podcast" on all things insurance sales and marketing.

Additionally, I offer non-contracted agents the opportunity to leverage my insurance sales training without contracting with me through the Insurance Agent Inner Circle Program, as well as through the Seminar Marketing Mastery program.

DAVID DUFORD

1. Seven Reasons Why Selling Insurance Is A Great Opportunity YOU Should Consider

In this chapter I'm going to share the seven reasons why I think selling insurance is a great opportunity.

Maybe you're reading my book because you're considering selling insurance, but you're not sure if it's right for you. Perhaps you're unhappy with your current career, and want to know more about the business.

For many that fully commit to the insurance sales business, there comes a level of freedom combined with the income-making ability that few people ever achieve.

Having been in life insurance sales since 2011, I want to share why I believe selling insurance is a phenomenal career opportunity that can provide for some, a level of freedom combined with an income-making ability that few people ever achieve.

#1 Reason to Sell Insurance: Freedom

When I started selling life insurance the final expense niche, I did well at first, but eventually struggled to the point of failure at the end of my first 12 months.

In order to survive and put food on the table, I had to get a job. Ironically, since my only other occupation was owning a personal training business, I didn't understand what it was like to have a "real" job. I took for granted the things that I had as a business owner, one of which was the freedoms gained from being your own boss.

Perhaps you all will understand my quandary better than I did at the time. Once you've owned a business, going to work for someone other than yourself is the opposite of freedom.

It's crazy! You're required to report to your desk at a set time each day. You're required to do certain tasks, report to certain people, and follow certain rules. While I sold for a reputable Fortune 500 company, I had to force myself to sell an inferior product I didn't believe in.

These realities of employment - that working for a company was not all it was cracked up to be - frustrated me to no end. There wasn't a day that I regretted the position I ended up in as an employee of someone else. Despite quitting the business, I realized my salvation from employment could still arrive through restarting insurance sales, where I could sell a product I wholeheartedly believed in.

If you polled all successful insurance agents, most would agree that freedom is one of the top benefits of the business. Many insurance agents have complete freedom to choose the product mix they offer their clients. Insurance agents have the ability to sell to whom they want, wherever they want, whenever they want. This gives you total freedom to custom-tailor your business the way you want!

And this freedom allows you to self-actualize work beyond simply a "job." You're not stuck in a boring, tedious career that means nothing beyond paying your bills. Rather, insurance provides sales you the runway to merge your work with real significance.

The freedom to work how you want, when you want, with whom you want is incredible! If you don't like what you do, selling insurance is a 180-degree difference. I don't have to sacrifice who I am, what it is that I do, who I believe. If I sell for a company that I don't like, well... screw them! I don't have to sell for them. I'm going to sell for somebody else.

#2 Reason to Sell Insurance: Wealth

Wealth is more than just your income and assets. To me, wealth is a measurement of the quality of your life.

Here's how I mean. Experiencing success in the insurance business has earned me the opportunity for more time with my children. I have four kids. Unlike a lot of people who work for someone else, I am lucky for the opportunity to be around my children every day of the week. I know what's going on in their lives. I'm there for them whenever they need me. I have a wonderful relationship with my wife. I'm always near her. Work does not get in the way my life and my relationship with my wife.

I have a wealth of relationships with clients and agents. Because of how demanding work is for many, relationships with those important people often are on the backburner. And even if the money is good for many in top employment positions, life is impoverished from relationships that, though they really matter, never get attention.

My point is this. These things are more important than the money! Of course, money does matter (and it's actually one of the great reasons to get into insurance) but it isn't top of the list for me. Remember, your time has value too!

#3 Reason to Sell Insurance: Income Opportunity

Selling insurance is truly one of those business models where the sky's the limit. You can achieve as high of an income as you want. It all depends on your work ethic, goals, and commitment level.

Though I've moved into recruiting and building a national agency, I still sell insurance. I make a very good income, so much so that I no longer have to worry about the basics of life - food, rent, taking care of my family - like I did very early on in my career.

If your main goal is to simply not be poor, to get away from that fear of how you will pay the bills - then selling insurance is a great option. If you want to be income-rich and you want to have more money than you know what to do with, following the right process for long enough will lead you to opportunity. So if you're looking to make more money, insurance is something that can definitely provide that.

#4 Reason to Sell Insurance: Make a Difference in People's Lives

Life insurance is a very unusual product. Most products that provide immediate gratification. But life insurance is in many ways meaningless to the person who buys it. It's truly their loved ones that benefit because in most cases it only benefits when the insured dies.

It's incredible to see what happens when that piece of paper comes to life when someone passes away. I could share countless examples of my clients' families realizing their parent's funeral is completely taken care of. It's awesome. You get the satisfaction of knowing you're helping everyday Americans who would not be able to afford the high cost of cremation or burial if it weren't for the policy you sold their loved one.

The same can be said for car insurance. How many people have had their cars totaled because of a drunk driver or text-messaging driver? And because of that insurance, they are able to replace an important piece of their lives.

For retirees, when the stock market crashes, their annuities never lose a penny. That's what insurance can do. Make a difference in people's lives. As an agent you are in a sense a superhero! Selling insurance gives you the ability to "save the day" when your clients and their loved ones need rescuing.

However, you won't see the beauty of your work initially. Some of your prospects will tell you they're not interested. They'll slam the door in your face. There's no getting around it. But the nice thing is that the people that you do sell to become your biggest fans, especially when they experience a loss. You make a huge difference in their lives. So if you want meaningful work that makes a difference in people's lives, insurance certainly does it.

#5 Reason to Sell Insurance: Activity-Based Success

Your success in the insurance business is primarily activity-based. In other words, selling insurance isn't rocket science. You don't have to be top of your class with three business degrees. You simply have to commit to the work and work hard.

For the most part, insurance sales products are pretty simple to understand. I always recommend new agents pick one product to master. Couple that with a lot of activity - seeing a lot of people, giving a lot of presentations, and asking them for their business - with enough time, you will see success.

So if you failed high school, don't have a college degree, or aren't necessarily the smartest person around, don't worry! I know many successful agents who make six-figure incomes who didn't attend school or only have a GED. None of their clients could care where they went to school, because how you connect and help matters way more than some academic piece of paper.

#6 Reason to Sell Insurance: Systematic Sales

The insurance sales business - no matter what type of product you want to sell - operates best as a holistic system. In many ways, selling insurance is a "rinse and repeat" process, combining systems of marketing, selling, and service. It's rudimentary. It's rote. It's repetitive. It doesn't take a lot of creativity for success. Just a lot of personal discipline to stick to the system.

#7 Reason to Sell Insurance: Simply Follow the Roadmap

Success in the insurance sales business is not a big secret. The road to success has already been paved. All you have to do is follow it!

Every insurance product available to sell has a corresponding sales and marketing system that someone has already tested and achieved success with. All you have to do as a new agent is to duplicate the system for yourself.

Your biggest responsibility as a new agent is to find an agent or agency that will teach you a sales and marketing system you can deploy on your own. There is zero reason to come up with some newfangled lead or sales presentation or any of that. Simply duplicate what's proven to work!

In fact, people like me who recruit agents nationally recognize this. We already have the sales and marketing system in place for the insurance products we sell. I'm not looking for a new agent to come in and reinvent the wheel. What gives us agency owners the best result is recruiting agents who will follow our sales and marketing system that's proven to deliver the best opportunity for results. You just have the humility and discipline to do what you're told!

2. How To Avoid Failing Out Of The Insurance Business

Ready for some harsh reality about selling insurance?

One of the dirty truths of the insurance business is that almost all new agents fail and leave the business within their first 12 months.

That's incredible (and horrific) if you think about it. How many industries can survive with 90% of new hires exiting the business in their first year? Not many, that's for sure.

Naturally, this leads us to the question: Why is failure so common in insurance sales? And how can you avoid the common pitfalls that snag most new agents?

Despite what many insurance agency recruiters say, selling any type of insurance is difficult. And yes, the odds are stacked against you.

In this chapter, I will detail my experiences as a personal producer and manager why agents fail, and give you actionable advice on how you can prevent failure from happening to you.

An important note: my thoughts on this subject is not a panacea preventing you from adversity. Many of you reading this will fail out of insurance sales, especially if you refuse to seek help from a mentor, and to learn from your mistakes.

To an extent, mass failure is simply the nature of this business. But I do believe IF you can learn from other's mistakes (like my own), you stand a better chance of achieving success.

Either way, if you decide to jump into this business, you need knowledge and preparation for what's to come. If you decide you don't have what it takes, that's fine. There's nothing wrong with knowing what's best for you. It's better than leaving this business economically worse off than you were when you started.

#1 Reason Agents Fail - Lack of Training

One of the biggest reasons why agents fail is a lack of sales, marketing, and product training.

If you haven't looked at insurance sales jobs yet, understand that most organizations follow a mass-recruiting, multi-level marketing strategy, similar to AVON, Herbalife, and Amway. Simply put, many insurance organizations recruit anyone under any circumstances, and focus their training more on how to get new recruits to recruit friends and family, instead of how to sell insurance.

This strategy is problematic. Why? Ultimately, if you have no experience actually selling insurance, who are you to bring on other people? Most of your recruits will discern that you have little to offer and will walk away. As a new agent, you should actively look for an insurance agency that will place training you in the craft of selling and marketing for insurance business above all else.

What does a good training system consist of? Good training consists of hands-on learning combined with self-study resources like scripts, combined with opportunities to "course correct" with the help of a trusted mentor. While you have to "sh*t or get off the pot" eventually, it's typically not in your best interest to be "thrown to the wolves" without prior training and preparation.

In persuasion careers like insurance sales, you must learn what to say, how to say it. Understanding your product's unique selling points is vital, and understanding how to communicate those points in easy-to-understand language is crucial. If you don't get this type of training upfront, your likelihood of failure increases exponentially.

Moral of the story - get trained up first before jumping into action.

#2 Reason Agents Fail - No Mentorship

Learning to sell insurance is very similar to apprenticing as a skilled laborer. If you want to get really good at selling insurance, you must spend time with a master insurance salesman.

While you don't need daily interactions with a coach or a mentor, you do need to have somebody who understands where you are in your career, and can offer custom-tailored advice on what elements of your skillset you need to improve.

Without mentorship, you're in a bad spot! Not having guidance, especially as a new agent, is hazardous to a new agent long-term potential in the business.

#3 Reason Agents Fail - No System of Success

All insurance agencies that do an excellent job recruiting agents and training them have a predefined procedure they use to teach new agents like you about selling and marketing their specific insurance product. These agencies understand that having a "track to run on" is paramount to quickly understanding the insurance sales process.

What if an agency hires you and has no formalized process of training new agents? Is this a big problem? In my experience talking with agents, an agency that fails to have a system to success is an agency that is on a collision course with failure. Any business without a process to train its people is destined to failure.

Many agencies - big and small - will hire new agents without a defined process of training them into capable producers. As a new agent, take caution of these operations. Many have no clue what they are doing, and they certainly won't know what to do with you when you jump on board. Long-term, they will have a hard time keeping agents, and will eventually crash and burn.

Pro-tip! Before joining an agency, look for evidence of success. See if there is an established training protocol. Good agency owners will jump at the opportunity to explain how their system of success takes coachable agents and turns them into consistent producers.

These are both things that your agency should exhibit before you think about joining them.

#4 Reason Agents Fail - Misplaced Priorities

Recruiting vs Producing

As you begin your career in insurance sales, you must define what you want to accomplish as a producer. Most of you are considering a career as a field agent selling insurance. And some want to recruit. That's fine. Figure out what you want to accomplish and then seek out an agency that shares the same values as you.

3. How to Reduce The Chances Of Failure

Now that I've covered the most common reasons that insurance agents fail in their first 12 months, let's discuss what steps you can take to prevent failure happening to you. Let's dig a little deeper on actionable steps you can take to take action on the four steps listed above.

#1 - Vet Your Options

When you're looking at joining an insurance agency, make sure you take time to interview the agency. That's right, actually interview your interviewer! Remember, the agent is the core of an agency's success, and you need to make sure the agency is a good fit for you.

The following questions are great to ask on every interview:

What is your training program like?

Who is successful in your organization? How are they successful?

What kind of system do they follow?

Can I do a ride along to see what they do?

What does a typical day look like?

How the agency recruiter answers will tell you a lot regarding whether the agency is worth joining. As an agency owner,. I'm more than happy to answer questions, but some agency owners get weirded out when they see an agent knows the deal. And you can judge the character of the organization very quickly based on "reading between the lines" of the answers.

As long as you're asking questions from a place of integrity, any negative pushback you receive is a good sign your recruiter operates a poorly-run agency.

#2 - Find a Producer-focused Organization

This is really important. You must first learn to sell the product you're interested in. Then, only after mastering the product, should you consider recruiting insurance agents into your agency. Likewise, stay away from recruitment-focused agencies that do not prioritize your skill development.

These organizations say they want production, but the focus is exclusively on teaching you recruitment tactics. This ultimately leads to failure because agents simply aren't trained to handle the realities of prospecting and selling insurance. They leave insurance sales thinking, "Oh, this whole business is just one giant multi-level marketing scheme. It's a pyramid scheme and a scam."

Spend your effort finding a mentor with first-hand experience marketing and selling insurance. When I was new selling final expense, I trained with an experienced agent who regularly placed $15,000 to $20,000 in final expense a month, netting approximately $150,000 a year after expenses. I learned how to hone in my script, how to handle objections, and how to run my business systematically. I wish every agent could have that kind of mentorship starting off. It was bountiful, in my beginning stages, to have that kind of access to a good producer.

#3 - Ask If They Have a System

Systems are everything in the insurance business. You need to find someone who can teach you his sales and marketing system. Who can recite it by heart. Who understands the process. Not somebody who teaches by the cuff, randomly, without any sort of a specific step-by-step procedure. If that's the case, you're just going to be thrown to the wolves and end up failing, another statistic.

Conclusion - Take Your Time

When it comes to looking for an agency to join, take your time. Failure is highly likely for many of you out there. But you can minimize the chances of failure, if you follow the steps discussed.

Sometimes agents fail, simply because they do not have what it takes to succeed. And that's okay. The important thing is to optimize everything that you can to help yourself have the best chance of success. Too many victims of failure in this business fail because of bad organizations, bad training, and bad coaching. Which is all totally preventable if you carefully look for the right agency from the outset of your career.

How To Determine Which Insurance Product Is Best To Sell

In this chapter, I'll describe the different product lines available to sell. This chapter is perfect for those of you interested in selling insurance, but aren't quite familiar with the various opportunities and markets to prospect for business. By the end of this chapter, you'll have more clarity in what insurance product you want to sell.

4. Life Insurance
What is life insurance?

Life insurance provides money into the hands of a beneficiary (a person/company/charity designated to receive the life insurance benefit) when the insured person dies.

Life insurance comes in all different shapes and sizes. Truly, there are dozens of niche-based functions for life insurance, depending on the market or group of prospects you target. For example, I sell burial insurance. Unlike targeting the income-replacement market, where clients buy six- and seven-figure death benefit policies, burial insurance (or final expense) policies are typically small in death benefit ($25,000 and less), designed to pay for final expenses like a burial or cremation.

Unlike targeting middle-class prospects and up, final expense burial insurance clientele are retired, draw a small Social Security check, and are on a fixed income. They buy burial insurance because they haven't the means to save enough money to pay for a funeral or cremation.

Of course, burial insurance is only one type of life insurance. Products such as mortgage protection term insurance are sold to middle-aged individuals in the workforce, wanting to pay off their home if they die unexpectedly.

There are also life insurance products that act similar to securities like stocks, yet protect the insured from stock market losses. This life insurance product is known as Indexed Universal Life. This insurance product is appealing to people who want a unique way to save for retirement, much like a 401k or IRA provides, and appreciate the added protection the life insurance product provides.

Pros And Cons Of Selling Life Insurance

The biggest advantage to selling any life insurance product is a high first-year commission. Even with smaller commission payouts like burial insurance, there are new agents making six-figure incomes after expenses. Same goes with mortgage protection term insurance and indexed universal life.

The drawback to selling life insurance. Little to no renewal-driven income. While life insurance provides a lucrative first-year income, the renewal income is paltry. Most products do not have a substantially high enough renewal for you to be able to live exclusively that income. If your goal is to create a semi-passive income through life insurance, the best path to do so is through agency-building.

One of the biggest benefits of selling insurance is the ability to create passive income streams with the right selection of insurance products. Right now, I can name off a handful of agents and agency owners who earn six- and seven-figure incomes from their renewal-based insurance production. Beyond servicing any call-ins from their clients, the work necessary to keep that business on the books is little to nothing. These agents make that kind of money before they roll out of bed.

Health Insurance

Let's talk briefly about health insurance, specifically the "Under 65" market. This market consists of the working public that needs health insurance to cover medical expenses.

Simply put, the opportunity to earn a living in the Under 65 health insurance market is virtually gone. Up to the early 2000s, selling Under 65 health insurance was lucrative. But with the Affordable Healthcare Act, most of that market went away.

While the business is not completely dead, I believe the opportunity for success is so low that targeting this market is largely a fool's errand. Luckily, there still is an opportunity in the health insurance market targeting the 65 And Older market, otherwise known as the Medicare market..

Medicare Insurance

You might think that Medicare covers all medical expenses. The truth is that it does not. While Medicare provides good coverage for seniors 65 and older, coverage is not comprehensive, which leads Medicare agents to the opportunity to sell additional coverage to better cover Medicare's gaps.

There are two primary plans to supplement what Medicare does not pay for. The first is called "Medicare Supplement." Depending on the type of Medicare Supplement purchased, the insured covers a large portion of what Medicare alone does not cover. The second type of plan is called "Medicare Advantage." This is a newer type of plan that alters what Medicare alone normally does so as to offer a more comprehensive policy to the insured. Most agents sell both products (although some will only specialize in one) to maximize sales.

Pros And Cons Of Selling To The Medicare Market

Selling Medicare Advantage and/or Medicare Supplements allow you to derive a renewal-based, passive income.

With enough time and effort, you may be able to generate a six-figure passive income from Medicare sales. For example, both Medicare Advantage and Medicare Supplement pays approximately a $250 to $300 annual renewal to agents. If you write 200 new policies for 5 years, you'll have 1,000 plans on the books, and you're probably going to make $250,000 to $300,000 in net income.

So why doesn't every new agent jump right into the Medicare market? The main reason is that the first few years selling Medicare tends to be the toughest. Since Medicare policies offer strong renewals, typically the first-year income isn't that hot. So an independent agent writing Medicare policies and paying for his leads will have a paltry income for a few years until his policy renewals kick into high gear.

The first year or two as a Medicare agent is the most difficult. You've got to overcome the expense of finding people to do business with you, which is a lot harder than you think. Perhaps you're thinking to yourself, "Well, I don't want to invest in marketing. I'll just cold call, knock on doors, and ask for referrals instead." Sure, you can do all of those things. Just understand that route is typically slower to gain traction.

Is there another way to get into Medicare sales? What most agents do is start in another niche like life insurance, then slowly transition over to Medicare sales. While this strategy can take a few years, it is a better strategy for many as it allows you time to save money from your life insurance sales and make the transition over with less financial worry. Alternatively, some agents choose to cross sell Medicare policies like I teach my final expense agents, as final expense prospects are commonly Medicare prospects, too.

Property and Casualty Insurance

Property and casualty insurance consists of policies that help cover losses associated with property such as your car and home, and casualty insurance covers in situations like accidents where you're held legally responsible.

A big advantage of selling property and casualty insurance is that government mandates ownership in most states for auto insurance. This means that everyone is literally a prospect! However, property and casualty insurance is renewal driven like Medicare, so it takes a bit of time before you develop a large renewal income.

As a life insurance agent looking from the outside in, selling property and casualty insurance seems more difficult to start up as an independent agent. Most P&C agents start their careers in well-known brands as captive agents, and discover they do not own the book of business they create. Instead, policies written belong to the agency, and if lucky, the agent must spend years committed to the organization before they own the block of business and any income streams it throws off.

Starting your career hand-cuffed, where your building someone else's business, isn't a smart long-term strategy for the agent interested in building a business. However, one could argue that getting sales and marketing training might justify the costs of not owning your business. But it remains that if you want to own your business versus building someone else's, you should look for P&C opportunities that vest you 100% in your block of business immediately, so that your clients and those income streams are yours, and not the agency's.

Take for example my auto insurance agent. I've kept coverage with her over 10 years now, and each year my policy produces an on-going flow of income for her. Unfortunately, because she was a captive auto insurance agent, she had to buy out her contract before fully owning my business. Had she not done that, she would've made substantially less off of my account in commission, and quite possibly have lost it altogether to the incumbent agency that originally owned the book.

Annuities

Let's talk about a growing part of the life insurance market that deals with helping our clients secure their financial goals.

An annuity is a life insurance product designed to protect the client's money from principal loss while also providing a level of interest. Annuities are used as a "safe money strategy" for many people. In my agency, we market annuities to senior citizens concerned about the risks of stock market crashes who want to ensure they do not outlive their retirement money.

There's incredible value in telling our annuity prospects, "We can give you some interest on your money, but more importantly we can protect you so that you never have to lose another penny if the stock market takes a wrong turn." Selling annuities offers very high first-year driven commissions for insurance agents. You can make four to six figures plus on one case depending on big the policy is.

Group Sales

The last point discussed in not so much a product as it is a market worth serious consideration as a new agent.

Selling insurance to groups allows you to take many of the concepts mentioned previously and scale it to help employers offer benefits to their employees. This scaling effect increases new business production, and potentially increases your average production per hour. The idea behind this business model is that one person gets to enroll lots of different people at once. Your profitability comes from a multi-policy sale as opposed to selling one person at a time.

I partner with an organization that sells life insurance to large employers. Their process is simple. They solicit employee benefit coordinators, sell them on their service of benefits management, and write up interested employees on the life insurance product.

You can target both large and small groups alike. Plenty of opportunity exists in both markets. Plus you can sell a litany of insurance products, like group health insurance plans and what's called voluntary payroll deduct life insurance, where the employee pays 100% of the cost of the insurance.

Also, selling group products gives you an edge in cross-selling other products to the owners and upper management of the business, like key man coverage.

Which Product Is Right For You?

What you've read up to this point consists of a sampling of the most popular types of insurance products available to sell. This list is not complete. So, if you're overwhelmed by this list and still aren't sure what's right for you, that's fine. It's never easy to decide which product to sell for most new agents.

So how do you figure out which direction to take? Here's a few pointers as we conclude this chapter.

Length Of Sales Cycle

Are you more comfortable with a short- or long-term sales cycle? Much of the life insurance and Medicare business is a short-term, one-call presentation opportunity that almost always ends with a written policy if the client is qualified and interested in buying. Selling Medicare and life insurance usually are not conducive to a multi-step sales call opportunity like large employee group sales or annuities are.

With short sales cycles, you have the benefit of getting paid faster than multi-step sales call insurance products. However, although not always the case, the income earned on short-term sales cycles typically is less than products sold on long-term sales cycles.

Much of this will come down to how quickly you need money. Can you wait months to get paid on a big sale opportunity? Or do you need to make money yesterday? If money's tight like it was for me when I started final expense sales, you may want to start with a one-call close insurance product.

Additionally, selecting a product like life insurance or annuities with a first-year commission probably makes more sense to start with if you would struggle financially initially selling a renewal-driven product like Medicare or property and casualty insurance.

Both life insurance and annuities pay more per sale on first-year commission than renewal driven products like Medicare, healthcare, property and casualty, and auto insurance.

Which Insurance Market Do You Like Best?

Lastly, spend time researching the different market opportunities. Figure out what markets appeal to you. Some readers prefer selling in people's businesses versus a stranger's home. Others prefer selling seniors versus younger, working people. The good news is that all of these market opportunities - entrepreneurial businesses and small business owners, corporate America, seniors, working middle-class - all offer incredible opportunity. Your job is to find the one that you enjoy the most!

5. How To Determine What Agency Opportunity Is Best For You

Perhaps the biggest problem new insurance agents have is picking the best sales opportunity. Why? Because anyone who's done any due diligence will see an endless stream of insurance sales "opportunities," some of which seem legit, others not so much.

The truth is that new agents are confused or ignorant of how to judge the quality of an insurance sales opportunity. That's my primary reason why YouTube channel and books receive lots of attention, since transparency and guidance are lacking. New agents struggle to find the answers they need.

If you're a newer agent or thinking about getting into this business as a licensed insurance agent, no doubt you seek guidance on finding the perfect agency to partner with. In this chapter, I'll hopefully answer many of your questions regarding insurance agency opportunities. Let's jump right in.

Option #1 - Work for One Insurance Company

Working exclusively for one insurance company is the traditional career track in the insurance business. Let's say you're considering joining New York Life, Northwestern Mutual, or MetLife. These are companies where you solely work for and represent that one company. You are considered an employee, have an initial draw period, and receive bonuses beyond your commission rate on hitting production goals. You're offered the usual employee benefits, like retirement plans and health insurance.

One of the biggest advantages of working for one insurance company is leveraging the company's long-standing brand. Name-dropping your company helps with your prospecting and selling efforts. While it varies from each branch office, most organizations offer detailed sales and prospecting training opportunities, both in classroom-sessions and one-on-one shadowing opportunities.

Despite the short-term advantages of working in a one-company career tract, there are drawbacks. First, commission maximization is difficult. One-company programs usually start you at half the commission level you'd receive as an independent, multi-carrier agent. Sure, one-company carriers will claim their bonus structure makes up for it. But the problem is that bonus structures are subject to change. At the whim of a new corporate "initiative," your new bonus structure may discourage production from your favorite product to sell, and require you to sell something else.

For example, many one-company property and casualty companies now require agents to sell life insurance to qualify for quarterly bonuses. In my experience, most P&C agents begrudge selling life insurance; they "stay in their lane" and sell what they know, which is car insurance and homeowners insurance. Imagine exceeding your targets on new P&C business written, only to lose your bonus payout because you didn't sell a few life insurance policies. Lame!

Perhaps one of the biggest disadvantages of selling for one company is **not** being vested in your book of business. "Vesting" means ownership. If you are not vested, you do not own your book of business. If you leave the company, your clients legally remain the company's You lose any income streams in renewals and as-earned commission you would have earned. This situation is the opposite of owning a business; instead, **you** are owned! All those clients, and all that income stream you built, gets shifted to the company, and now you start at Square 1.

Since I am a vehement entrepreneur and practically unemployable, this particular point was enough reason for me to avoid investigating most one-company opportunities. If I prospect for new business myself, I do not want to either (a) lose my renewal income stream, or (b), get shut out due to non-competes from my clients. Corporate priorities change. New management comes and goes. While change can help your business, it can also hurt if management is shortsighted. The point is, my business is at their mercy, at all times. This is why I did not choose this career path when I entered the insurance sales business.

Option# 2- Work for Many Companies Simultaneously

Working for one company is not the only career route into selling insurance. In fact, one-company representation is the extreme minority, with approximately 20% of insurance agents partnering with a singular insurance company.

Nowadays, partnering with multiple insurance companies is the most popular route. In short, I also refer to multi-company partnering as being an independent agent. As an independent agent, I associate with as many carriers as I please (as long as they'll appoint me). And I do this in order to give my insurance prospects more and better program options to choose from.

Here's why. Unlike in the retail world where all you need to buy a product is money, insurance companies won't cover any person, even if they can afford it. Instead, insurance carriers require applicants for insurance to qualify according to its underwriting standards. And those underwriting standards vary from carrier to carrier.

Let me provide a few examples to clarify my point, as this is the foundation to why so many new agents choose the independent, multi-company career path when starting. I sell final expense life insurance. My prospects are fixed-income seniors. How well their health is in combination with their age has a direct impact on eligibility and the premium. If I partner with one company, I must force-fit every prospect into that one company, even if the premium is overpriced or the coverage is inferior to other options.

The same goes for car insurance. Applicants may have recent moving violations, DUIs, or recent claims history. Even living in certain parts of the country affects your premium. So why force fit all your clients into one company that may not offer the best coverage package?

The implications for force-fitting are dramatic. First, you will not sell as many of your prospects that earnestly need help. This means you'll make less and leave your prospects without coverage they dearly need. Second, for a portion of your prospects, you increase the risk of lapses and chargebacks. Imagine losing a client because another agent swooped in and offered a better deal. Guess what? It happens all the time, especially to agents who don't offer multiple carrier options.

Of course, selling with multiple insurance companies is not always rainbows and sunshine. As with singular-company representation, there are drawbacks to multi-company representation.

First, access to sales and marketing training is hit or miss. While some multi-carrier agencies like mine are heavily focused on training, many are not. They are simply places to get carrier appointments. So if you knew sales and marketing training (and you definitely do if you're new to the business), then take time to ask about the level of training provided.

Second, for some, learning multiple carriers simultaneously is overwhelming. Yes, the learning curve is steeper than learning one company's product. However, that is simply the price you must pay, if you want to maximize your sales opportunities.

Option #3 - Work With A Multilevel Marketing Company

If you though multi-level marketing was for make-up and cookware, think again!

While there are no insurance sales organizations that proudly exclaim that they're multi-level marketers, the multi-level marketing process and mindset is alive and well in insurance sales. However, the key point I want you to take away is to understand how to identify those organizations that have the MLM mindset, first and foremost.

Before we go further, multi-level marketing refers to organizations that use sales reps to recruit other reps (also known as downlines) to continue the selling and recruiting process. This creates a structure similar to a pyramid. Most folks aware of multi-marketing are either in love with the concept, or despise it. Why? Because multi-level marketers tend to be full of hype, and notoriously bother their friends and family to either join or buy from them.

In the insurance business, while the hierarchy of recruiting downlines and building agencies is similar to multi-level marketing, the MLM mindset varies from organization to organization. Structurally, insurance carriers have "outsourced" the recruitment and training responsibilities to large, national marketing organizations and their syndicates below them, such as agencies and field agents. This is similar in design to the traditional multi-level marketing structure.

But here's the thing. Just because the design is similar, doesn't mean that the organization you're apart of will be a typical MLM experience you're probably familiar with. There are insurance organizations like mine that do not adhere to typical mindset of "Kool-Aid drinking" and showing off Rolexes and sports cars. Those organizations and agencies typically are the better ones to consider joining, as the focus is more on skill development as a producing agent, as opposed to hyping you up in some rah-rah meeting.

How can you tell if the insurance sales opportunity you're considering has a MLM mindset? The biggest giveaway is if they focus more on recruiting than producing. Once you talk to the recruiter, and especially if you attend the meeting, you'll know for sure if said-company is an MLM if they spend a good chunk of the time talking about how building a downline is the answer to making money in the insurance business, while sharing stories of other downlines who've made a lot of money. Also, many MLMs advertise heavily on online job boards like ZipRecruiter and Monster.

What if your goal is to build an agency? If you don't care about the shortcomings of not having a focus on training you to become a skilled producer first, then join the MLM. However, if you care more about becoming a competent and skilled producer first and foremost before going down the agency-building route, be wary about joining the MLM. You'll likely find that doing so is a serious mismatch and will not provide the resources necessary, much less the culture needed to achieve your goals.

Option #4 - Work for a Producer-Focused Organization

A producer-focused organization devotes itself to finding and recruiting agents who are open-minded, have faith and humility, and want to duplicate a sales and marketing system to actually SELL insurance versus recruiting insurance agents.

Advantages to aligning with a producer-based organization are obvious. Producer-focused organizations are all about developing agents into competent and independent producers. They provide sales and marketing programs, as well as lead programs. You may or may not have to pay for the leads. Either way, producer-focused organizations dedicate themselves to your success in the field.

Drawbacks to this arrangement are minimal. I guess if your life's mission is to recruit without regard to having actual experience selling the product, then maybe a producer-focused agency isn't for you. You'll find in many producer-oriented organizations, recruiting is either discouraged or not encouraged. If your long-term strategy is to recruit and the organization does not support your vision, you may want to consider an eventual exit for better horizons.

Land Mines to Dodge

When you are searching for your first insurance company to partner with, there are a number of "landmines" to avoid. Here are some suggestions to make the search for an agency go a little easier.

#1 - Define Your Goals and Stick to Them

Above all else, avoid agent-agency misalignment. How do you do it? Take a personal inventory of what's important to you in an insurance sales career. Ask questions like:

What do you want to get out of your career?

Do you want to recruit?

Do you want to exclusively sell?

What insurance products do you want to sell?

What markets are you interested in?

What level of support do you require?

Think through all of these questions. Answer them as thoroughly as possible. Obviously plans can change, but having an end-point in mind eliminates many of the snags new agents experience.

One other reason to do your personal self-assessment is to fend off the many mass-recruiting operations that hire anyone with a pulse.

Everybody is a prospect to them, and you must tread carefully, as they will attempt to convince you that their "secret sauce" is exactly what you need.

#2 - Look for Transparency

When interviewing with an insurance agency, take note at how management responds to your questions. One takeaway I hope you experience from reading this book is the knowledge of what questions to ask when interviewing for an insurance sales position. Good management will respond courteously and in detail to any question you pose. Plus, they'll respect you for doing your due diligence.

If you get snarky and short answers to your questions, or if the interviewer doesn't answer with a good-faith effort, likely something is amiss. Perhaps they are bullheaded and obstinate to work with. Or maybe they typically operate with agents in the dark, and prefer not to hire agents with preliminary knowledge. Either way, my experience is this; any other response other than a straightforward answer is a red flag, a sign that should prompt you to walk away and find insurance sales work somewhere else.

#3 - Office Culture

If you're joining a traditional agency with a local office, it is smart to observe the office culture before joining. Insurance agencies with local offices should value their employee work culture.

Observe how employees interact with each other. Is there camaraderie? Is there a spirit of success and hard work ethic?

My first sales job in college was with a real estate agency. After I received my real estate license, I visited the local office that leased apartments to students. Walking into the office, I immediately sensed a feeling of despair. None of the agents looked up from their desks to greet me. And this was before smartphones occupied everyone's attention. To make matters worse, the owner of the organization was a real jerk. Always screaming, yelling, and insulting others. Clearly the company culture of misery trickled from the top to the bottom. Needless to say, this work environment shocked me.

Instead of working in a doom-and-gloom work environment, see out an agency supportive of your successes. While I'm not advocating a rainbows and sunshine, Kumbaya-fest, you do want an environment built around helping you succeed and lifting you up.

Last point - trust your instincts! If you're Spidey-senses are tingling after your interview, you should probably listen.

#4 - Patience!

Finally, be patient! You may be raring' to go and sell some insurance, but don't let your drive to enter the business cause you to make a faulty agency partnership selection. Patiently do your research first. Look for multiple agencies with shared alignment and interview them all. With more time to investigate the opportunities, the better your odds to find insurance sales success, right out of the gates!

DAVID DUFORD

6. Elements Necessary To Achieve Success In Insurance Sales

A Crash Course.

Here's the truth about selling insurance...

Somewhere between 90% and 95% of newly licensed insurance agents FAIL out of the insurance sales business within the first 12 months of starting their new career. That means only 1 or 2 out of 20 agents survive into their second year. That's crazy!

You should strive to not only survive, but thrive selling insurance! Doing so does not require magic superpowers or inherent talent. There are several factors you need to embrace to improve your odds of first-year and life-long career success in insurance sales. As a YouTube creator for insurance sales and marketing training since 2014, I've had the privilege of interviewing a number of successful agents. And the one similarity shared by all is having a champion's mindset.

I believe having a champion's mindset is critical for your success, no matter what insurance product your sell. And today I'll discuss the 6 factors I've seen all top producers share that you must emulate now, if you want a fighting chance to succeed in selling insurance.

#1 - Coachability

Coachability is key. Accept that you know little to nothing about your new insurance career. Embrace the curiosity of a child, and accept guidance and correction from you superiors who have already traveled the same path.

When I first began selling final expense life insurance, I knew nothing about in-home sales. Thankfully, I was paired with a top-producing mentor named Andrew in Atlanta, who I learned the basics of the business. I was taught how to door knock my final expense leads to present on the spot, and how to give a results-oriented presentation that would convert prospects into happy buyers. Instead of reinventing the wheel, I took his system and duplicated it in my territory. And within a matter of weeks, I started seeing results.

Sales trainer Brian Tracy teaches us that all top producers started at the bottom. Have comfort in this as you begin your insurance sales journey, as this means top producers learned their way to the top through the same process you did!

Remember that you'll make mistakes. Every top producer made mistakes along the way. Suppress your ego from turning your heart away from constructive criticism necessary to overcoming your weaknesses. It's in these moments of vulnerability you'll find opportunities for newfound growth and development. Coachability is something we have to have in order to grow ourselves upward, outward and toward the direction of continual success.

#2 - Have Humility

Humility must exist before one can experience advances in skills and personal development. In a sense, it is the opposite of ego. Ego blinds you from self-improvement and seeing things for the way they are. Ego provides a false sense of assurance, contributing only to your ultimate demise. Do not let your ego lead you. Have the humility and honesty with yourself that you do not have all the answers. This shouldn't lower your self-confidence; it should raise it! Humility is recognition of your imperfections, and an understanding that you can change things to better yourself

Early in my career, my ego disrupted (thankfully, only temporarily) my final expense life insurance career. Frustrated with dealing with deadbeat leads, I devised a way to completely eliminate wasting time with frustrating prospects that didn't buy, while spending all my time with buyers. Ultimately, the idea did not pan out, costing me more in time and lost opportunity than if I had used the original system I was taught.

The moral of the story was my ego shielded me from humbly accepting that there are elements to the business that one cannot ever overcome. All salespeople do not sell all prospects. In fact, spending time with non-buyers is a natural process to selling anything. Few have ever overcome it. And instead of following the sales and marketing system I was taught - and accepting the good AND the bad that comes with any sales and marketing process - I thought I knew better, ultimately costing me a year working in a job I hate before I could get back into the insurance business.

#3 - Have Faith

Faith is the glue that binds everything together. While I can show you proof that implementing an insurance sales and marketing process has produced six-figure income results for many of my agents, I can't guarantee that you will experience the same success. Ultimately, no one with integrity can guarantee you any kind of success in insurance sales. Nobody can replace you taking the same leap of faith we've all had to take to see if the insurance sales opportunity can work for us.

But what if you have doubts? That's totally normal. And probably a good thing, too. Doubt is a survival mechanism passed along over the ages. It prevented our ancestors from doing dumb things that could have ended their lives. Without a sense of doubt, you may not be here today!

Understand that doubt is a good thing, and that it's possible to have faith anyway. The key is to maximize our faith in ourselves while minimizing doubt. I do this by what I expose myself to. First, the best way to overcome doubt is to converse with people successful already in the insurance career you want to pursue. If you talk to enough people, you'll realize that many of those successful are not geniuses. Yes, they have the "it" factor, but many of them started in humble beginnings while embracing the concepts explained in this chapter.

Reading autobiographies and biographies about famous figures in history is surprisingly invigorating. Autobiographies especially provide a level of human insight to historical figures that originally appeared unshakable. My favorite 2 autobiographies that had the most impact on my career are Benjamin Franklin's autobiography, and "Growing Rich," by Randall Baskin. Both books illuminate how each individual started in difficult circumstances, yet overcame their difficulties with faith and commitment. I recommend both to you to develop a sense that it is possible to overcome and achieve, no matter your circumstances.

So... have faith to start. Have faith to continue, especially when things get tough. When you find the mentor, the coaching program, the sales and marketing system that aligns with your goals- everything you need to be successful - take that leap of faith that it will all work out. And keep it during times of difficulty.

#4 - Positive Outlook

A positive outlook on your current and future circumstances is critical. Why? Because all insurance salespeople deal with rejection. Prospects telling you they're not interested, they changed their mind, or flat-out telling you to go to hell. When you're out there selling, positivity is both the shield to protect yourself and the sword to win the battle. Maintaining positivity despite your circumstances keeps you attractive to those real prospects that actually want to buy what you're selling.

With positivity you'll exude enthusiasm. Be enthusiastic about what you're selling! Your success with insurance clients rests on your ability to move prospects emotionally moving toward your cause.

Needless to say, negativity has no place in selling insurance. Fight it with all your might. Prospects immediately pick up on your negative disposition, even if you think you're hiding it. And good prospects don't do business with negative salespeople. Nobody wants to do business with a Debbie downer.

#5 - Responsibility and Consistency

I explained earlier how selling insurance facilities a level of freedom few careers can offer. Understand that freedom is a two-sided coin. And to have freedom, one must shoulder the responsibility that accompanies it. In fact, you must embrace responsibility.

The more you can embrace responsibility for all of your circumstances - good AND bad - the better. Embrace the responsibility of prospecting and activity. Embrace taking care of your clients. Embrace doing what's necessary, even in adversity. Embrace getting cursed out for the fifth time in a row while door knocking. All of this is your responsibility as an insurance professional, IF you want the much-coveted freedom that comes along with this career.

You are responsible. The buck does not pass with you. You own it. All your problems and failures, and all of your success. It's all your responsibility. Embracing this belief makes life better and clarifying. Why? Because now YOU are in control of your destiny. You can dictate where you go in your life. Because YOU are responsible!

#6 - Discipline

Discipline applies to coachability, humility, faith, positivity, and responsibility. Discipline is vital, especially when you are your own boss. Every morning it's up to you to go to work. It's up to you to execute your plan no matter what. If you don't have discipline, you don't have a business. Period. You're just playing around. Yeah, maybe you'll help some people here and there, but you're not going to be as happy and as successful as you could be.

Conclusion

My hope is that this chapter clarifies in your mind how important developing your mindset is to your success selling insurance. Mindset is a part of everything you do, how you achieve goals, interact with prospects, and close sales. Remember! No one said selling insurance was going to be easy. But you certainly set yourself up for greater success when you adopt the mindset of a champion.

DAVID DUFORD

7. How To Get Your Insurance License

This chapter is specifically for agents who directions on studying and applying for an insurance license. You'll learn how to prepare and what to expect on the exam.

If you have already passed your insurance license exam, you can skip this chapter.

Each state regulates insurance law and licensing new insurance agents. And with each state operating according to its own rules, you'll need to use Google to research your state's requirements.

Thankfully, this is simple. Google-search "how to get licensed for insurance in [your state]", filling in [your state] with where you live. Each state has a licensing overview page that explains the process of preparing, testing, and applying for insurance license.

Complete A Pre-Licensing Course

Most states require you to pass a pre-licensing course prior to taking the official insurance exam. While some pre-licensing courses have classroom learning options, most agents opt for the internet-based home study version. Cost for pre-licensing ranges between $50 to $200, depending on the vendor and state you're testing in. Your state's Department Of Insurance will recommend the appropriate pre-licensing vendor to use.

How Much Time To Study?

I've seen motivated people complete pre-licensing in a week. On average, most people study 2 to 3 weeks prior to completing pre-licensing and taking the exam.

How Does Taking The Insurance Exam Work?

After completing pre-licensing, you're ready to take the official exam. You'll need to contact your state's testing provider and schedule a date. Refer to your state's Department Of Insurance directions for a list of preferred vendors.

Most insurance exams consist of 100 or so questions with a multi-hour time limit. Most finish well within the allotted time range.

What Kind Of Questions Are On The Exam?

Exam questions based on the study material you completed. Prior to the exam, continue to study according to your pre-licensing material.

What Happens After I Pass The Exam?

Once you pass, you can apply for your insurance license. Expect the state to conduct a background check. Remember, selling insurance is a privilege, not a right, so your state's DOI has ultimate say on whether or not you get a license.

Most states also require fingerprints. Again, refer to your state's DOI for direction on where to get fingerprints completed.

Do I Ever Have To Take Another Insurance Exam Again?

Once you pass the exam, that's it for testing for the specific license you tested for. While you never have to take another exam for that license, you will have to go through the same procedure laid out earlier if you want to add an additional insurance license.

For example, if you originally tested and acquired your life insurance license and want to sell health insurance, you'll have to study and test for the health insurance license prior to offering any form of health insurance to your prospects.

How Does Continuing Education Work?

Every 2 years, your state expects 24 hours' worth of continuing education completed, prior to renewing your insurance license. Thankfully, all state DOIs allow online-based continuing education course work that you complete at your own pace.

What If I Want To Sell In A State I Don't Live In?

All states recognize each other's licensed insurance agents, and allow non-residents to license to sell insurance. Once your home state licenses you, pay your non-resident licensing fee in the states you want, and in most cases, your approved to sell in those states within a few days. NIPR.com is the best place to start for non-resident insurance license applications.

8. How To Prepare For An Insurance Agent Job Interview

In this chapter, I'll explain how to prepare for an insurance interview to maximize your chances of getting the insurance sales job you REALLY want.

First, I'll discuss the "truth" about applying for insurance jobs, as there is air to clear. You'll learn what your insurance sales interviewer is looking for, and I'll end with advice on how you can positively differentiate yourself from applicants.

The TRUTH About Insurance Jobs

In most cases, interviewing for an insurance sales job is unlike interviewing for any other sales job. While most corporations carefully pick through applicants, most insurance agencies will hire anyone halfway presentable. In fact, the joke recruiters recite commonly include:

"Can you fog this mirror? You're hired!", and,

"Do you have a pulse? You're hired!"

Joking aside, the truth is this: many insurance agencies focus on the *quantity of agents hired*, not the *quality of agents hired*. In fact, many recruiting managers' bonuses depend partially on new recruitment volume.

The point is this: there is less emphasis put on resume quality and pedigree in new insurance agent recruitment than other non-insurance sales opportunities. However, that doesn't mean you shouldn't be prepared, as the better agencies tend to vet harder upfront.

The ONE Question To Prepare For

When called in to do your insurance sales interview, spend time preparing to answer the interviewer's question about "The Project 100".

What is the Project 100? Project 100 (or Project 200 in some agencies) refers to you listing the names of your friends, family, and business associates you'll call on for insurance sales presentations. Many brand-name insurance agencies you'll apply to teach their new agents to prospect their social network for sales opportunities, and want to know if your network is large enough to support you getting up and running.

When asked about your list of contacts, impress your interviewer and present a list of 100 to 200 names within your sphere of influence. Explain your relationship with each and how you plan on contacting them. This alone will convince many interviewers to hire you by your prior preparation alone.

What the Interviewer Looks for

Beyond the Project 100, agencies hiring quality over quantity will ask standard interview questions you're already familiar with if you've held a sales position. Either way, below I'll explain the most common concerns hiring managers have regarding new agent recruits, and how to best prepare answering their questions.

#1 - *Show Evidence of Past Success*

Selling insurance is hard. Success in insurance requires mental and emotional resilience. Hiring managers want recruits who will stick through difficulties, not quitters who leave when the going gets tough.

Consider your past employment, internships, or sporting activities. How can you describe moments of difficulty that you've overcome? Can you explain it in story-fashion? What did you learn from your adversity? Think through your life experiences and be able to deliver a powerful statement that proves your ability to fight off challenges. While any personal story of overcoming difficulties is great, if you have sales experience, focus your story on that. Evidence of success in overcoming obstacles in sales is huge.

#2 - *Show You Are a People Person*

Insurance sales is all about helping people solve problems. Empathy and a desire to serve your clients is critical to your long-term success. While too much empathy detracts from your closing capability, a complete lack of empathy prevents meaningful connection. Somewhere in the middle is good, a combination of both empathy and authority.

How do you show empathy? Describe your commitment to the people you served in your prior jobs, internships, or sports team affiliations. Explain in detail how you showed your concerns to your clients, employees, or teammates, and what effect that had on your experience and those that you served.

#3 - *Coachability*

This is huge! Your hiring manager wants to know if you're the type of hire that will take charge and execute on the sales strategies the agency teaches. Why? Because hiring someone who doesn't take action (or think he knows a better way) largely leads to the agent failing, directly impacting the bottom line of the agency.

One of the biggest reasons people fail at selling insurance is the agent's unwillingness to be coached. You must be open to constructive criticism from your managers and adjust your strategy accordingly.

You must make it clear to your hiring manager that you are COMPLETELY coachable. How? Have several stories prepared ahead of time explaining situations where a superior corrected you on a mistake you made. Explain how you responded, and what steps you took to improve.

#4 - Company Culture Match

Interviewers often focus on how well the new agent matches the agency's culture. Managers want to make sure your personality is a good fit for the company. Research ahead of time the company's culture to get an idea of how it works.

#5 - Differentiate Yourself From The Competition

Differentiation refers to your ability to explain how you are different than someone else. Interviewers are looking for the perfect match for their insurance agent position, so you must describe why picking you is their best choice relative to the other applicants. There are a number of ways to differentiate yourself from your interviewee competition. Here are a few suggestions:

Appearance Matters

On interviews, always dress in a suit and tie. Make sure your suit fits well and shoes are polished. Don't do what I did once - I bought a new suit, but forgot to cut the little white thing on the back. I looked like a complete dope. Simply ensure you look good and presentable. Pass on the cologne (could trigger an allergy). Make sure your breath doesn't stink. Sounds like common sense, but common sense isn't all that common. Interviewers appreciate when applicants pay attention to details, and making these fixes is easy to do and goes a long way in your favor.

Explain What Attracts You to Selling Insurance

Having a powerful answer to the question, "Why do you want to sell insurance?" is incredibly important. You must develop a succinct answer to this interview question.

Your answer must be better than, "I need the money." Put thought into what excites you about selling insurance. Why would you want to sell insurance over selling cars, or another sales position? Think of the benefits of insurance sales mentioned earlier in this book. Do any of them mean something to you? If so, share that!

For example, the reason I sell life insurance is because it allows me to have the freedom I want while helping everyday people.

Take time to understand why insurance is important to you. If possible, share a story about how an insurance product helped your family or loved one. For example, maybe you've lost a spouse, parents, grandparents, and you saw what it was like where there was life insurance or what it was like when there was no life insurance. Nothing sparks a desire to sell insurance more than experiencing what insurance does when needed. interviewers appreciate and understand that connection. That's what they're looking for ultimately - a personal connection or life story relating to insurance with passion behind it.

Take Time to Understand the Company Products and Demonstrate Basic Understanding

Many years ago, I interviewed with a uniform sales company. The interview went well. At the end of the interview, the hiring manager asked, "Do you have any questions for me?" I followed up with a half-dozen questions that delved deeper into the position, seeking clarity and direction on the opportunity.

You must anticipate this question at the conclusion of your interview. And when asked the question, NEVER answer, "No, I don't have any questions." That is, unless you DO NOT want the job. Instead, take the opportunity to ask questions about the company and a basic level of understanding of the product you'll sell if hired.

After my interviewer asked me to ask him questions, I asked about the company's competitiveness: "I understand your top two competitors are Cintas and UniFirst. How do you think Aramark is superior over Cintas and UniFirst?" The interviewer would answer and we'd share some back and forth regarding Aramark's competitiveness and strengths. Then I asked about the company's new product line investments: "It sounds like Aramark's making some big investments in the medical servicing field. What do you think about Cintas' new program they've rolled out to provide uniforms for surgical techs, and how do you think Aramark will stack up against it?" I impressed the interviewer with my understanding and preparation, and got the job.

If you take time to research, you'll discover much about the company you're interviewing. All the basic information about the company structure, product line, and strengths are readily available to those who care to look online. Further, ask agents working for the company on internet forums like Reddit and Facebook groups for insight. Go so far as to call a district office in another territory and say, "Hey, I'm doing an interview. What do you think are the best products you sell? What are your thoughts on what will impress this guy?" Just that little extra added step makes a big difference. It will totally differentiate you from the applicants uninterested in going the extra mile to prepare.

Always Ask for the Job!

Always ask for the job at the end of the interview. You don't have to be a hard closer, either. Simply ask for the position using the following language: "Well, Mr. Jones, based on this interview, do you think I'm the appropriate person for this position? Do you see any reason why you wouldn't hire me?" For hiring managers with sales experience, this is a big deal. An interview is essentially a sales presentation. And all sales presentations must end with you asking for the sale, right?

Summary

Following my advice should measurably help you increase your odds of getting the insurance job of your dreams. If you do everything I've described - presented yourself well, demonstrated your passion and knowledge of the insurance business and company, and asked for the position at the conclusion of the interview, the odds are thoroughly stacked in your favor.

DAVID DUFORD

9. A Track To Run On

In this chapter, I'll explain the importance of having a track to run on, following a sales process, and what happens when you don't.

I first learned the importance of a track to run on from New York Life Insurance agent, Ben Feldman. Ben is a legendary Guinness World Record holder for life insurance sales back in the '60s and '70s. He's gone now, but a great person to learn from, and he gave back a lot to the business, especially in the 2 books he wrote (buy them on Amazon).

Ben Feldman shared in his book, "The Feldman Method", the importance of having a track to run on. Here's how he meant. It's not enough just to have a license if you want success in the insurance business. What you really need to achieve success is clarity on what you want to sell, and the process of how you get to a sale. In other words, you must have a process in placing, putting you in front of prospects inclined to have an interest in what you're selling.

When I started in insurance, I studied several options and chose to sell final expense. Final expense is also called burial insurance. It's a simple product, targeted to low-income seniors 60 and older who are disabled or retired. I liked this market because there are millions of low-income seniors with few having savings to pay for their own funeral. It makes sense to sell as they have an inherent need for it. Bottom line, final expense offered clarity to me in opportunity to do well, given the market opportunity.

Better yet, I discovered final expense sales had been around for decades. Why was this important? Because other agents before me had already figured out works and what doesn't work. They had developed a process, a track to run on. There was no guesswork necessary on testing out the viability of the concept. The job was stable because it offered a process of generating leads interested in buying, and a sales strategy to persuade prospects to buy from me.

The reason I mention my experience as a new agent isn't necessarily to convince you to sell final expense. Not at all. Instead, it is to show you what factors to look for in an insurance sales opportunity. You MUST have a well-defined strategy to get you in front of prospects on a consistent basis if you want success. If you join an insurance agency that doesn't have a track to run on, be wary. You do not want to be the guinea pig in this science experiment.

What happens when you don't access to a sales and marketing system?

You fail. It's just a matter of time.

How do you find a track to run on? Due your due diligence. Interview multiple agencies. Find the one that has the best training, the best mentors, the best sales and marketing strategies. And when you find a good match, don't try to reinvent the wheel. Do what you're told! Be a good soldier when starting out. Good leaders start out as good followers.

10. Find A Mentor!

I can't emphasize enough the importance of finding an insurance mentor you like and can trust. Learning the craft of insurance is similar to the apprenticeship approach to learning trades of yesteryear. Back in the day a man would take his son into his business and teach him his trade (like carpentry). His son would apprentice for years, working with his father, improving his skills.

No matter what type of insurance product you sell or want to sell, learning the craft of selling insurance is exactly the same. You need a skilled veteran of the business to take you under their wing. This allows you to not only learn the best way to succeed, but also gives you the opportunity to learn the business the right way the first time around.

Don't make the same mistakes I made, starting and failing out because I thought I could do things my way. It took coming back a second time after learning from others who had much more experience than me for me to understand the importance of mentorship.

This is not a business you want to do on your own. Trust me. You may have the inclination or desire to go it alone and not want to work with somebody else, but having a mentor makes a dramatic difference.

You're going to learn faster, you're going to appreciate the nuances faster and really, long term, you're going to make more money.

11. Develop And Refine Your Sales Skills

One of the best things you can do to give yourself a chance at success is to develop your sales skills. It's really important to master the art and science of selling insurance. Words matter in this business. How you say what you say, and a well-developed presentation strategy is imperative for high levels of sales success.

What's the easiest way to develop your sales skills? Mimic what top producers do. Find top producer insurance agents in the market that interests you. Ask to do a ride-along to see how they sell. Many will oblige. Notice what top producers say, how they say it, and how they act with their prospects. You'll notice a consistency, an order, a process.

Another way to develop your sales skills? Find an organization specialized in training new insurance agents on their sales and marketing strategies. This is how my insurance agency works. I plug new agents into a sales and marketing system proven to work to sell products like final expense, Medicare products, annuities, and other insurance products. Having a proven sales and marketing system takes the guesswork out of selling. All you have to do is simply follow the directions.

12. Activity Is King

In this chapter, I will explain why activity is the cornerstone to your success in selling insurance, no matter what product you ultimately choose.

In 2018 at the 8% Nation Wealth Conference, I participated as a panelist speaker. Leading the conversation, Cody Askins asked me, "What is your advice to people who are struggling out in the field?" My response...

All sales woes come from a lack of prospecting!

Here's what I've discovered. Ninety percent of insurance agents struggling to make a living simply are NOT doing enough sales presentations. Not a lack of sales technique, but a lack of activity.

Sure. You can't be a moron in front of your prospects, of course. But while you can learn better sales scripts, more rebuttals, and better approaches, you cannot realize a profit from your training UNTIL you've done the hard work of prospecting to see enough people. Bottom line, "Seeing the people" is the most important factor in your success as an insurance agent. I'd wager 80% of your success comes from your activity level, and 20% from your sales technique.

How do you maximize your activity? First, you need to track all aspects of your activity attempts. Door knocks, phone calls, booked appointments, average profit per sale. Get to know your numbers. Once you do, you can extrapolate out what type of activity you must invest to yield the income you want.

The Magic Number 15

if you're full time, focus on completing 15 presentations a week. There's something about 15 weekly presentations I've heard from all sorts of top producers in different lines of insurance. Many agree that completing 15 appointments weekly has a kind of "magical" effect on consistency of production. Obviously it's not magic, but outcomes seem to become more stable with that level of activity. There's less swings in income, and agents are less stressed if the outcome of a presentation isn't a sale. When you're doing like 15 appointments a week, you care, but not that much. You want to help, but if they don't want it, you're just going to go onto the next one. What's the worry? You've got 14 more people to see.

What if you're not able to hit 15 appointments weekly? One reason is you're not getting enough leads. Not all leads will allow you to book an appointment. So work on filling the pipeline accordingly. Another reason is you're not working hard enough. Sometimes the difference between success and failure in this business is one more door knock, one more prospecting attempt, before calling it a day. Or maybe you need to start a little earlier, or work an extra day. Remember, this is the price EVERYONE pays for success. And you're no different.

Be MANIACAL about hitting your presentation goals. And break your weekly presentation goal into daily presentation goals Do NOT stop working until you hit your daily REQUIRED sales presentation quota. And when you do, your income will take care of itself.

DAVID DUFORD

For More Information

- Website: DavidDuford.com
- YouTube Channel: Search "David Duford" in YouTube
- Podcast Channel: In ITunes, search "The David Duford Show"
- Info On Joining David Duford's Insurance Agency: https://buylifeinsuranceforburial.lpages.co/david-duford-recruiting/ - or go to DavidDuford.com and click "Join Dave's Agency" in the top menu.
- David's Email: David@DavidDuford.com

DAVID DUFORD

Other Books by David Duford

1. The Official Guide To Selling Final Expense Insurance: Get the e-book on DavidDuford.com, or purchase on Amazon.

2. Interviews With Top Producing Insurance Agents: Get the e-book on DavidDuford.com, or purchase on Amazon.

3. The Official Guide To Selling Insurance For New Agents: Purchase On Amazon.

Made in the USA
Columbia, SC
24 February 2022

56799916R00067